10 DISCIPLINES OF A GODLY WOMAN

Barbara Hughes

10 > DISCIPLINES OF A GODLY WOMAN

Discipline seems like a hard word, but discipline is your lifeline, something that you learn to embrace and thank God for as you grow in him.

The apostle Paul links the idea of discipline with spiritual life: "Train yourself for godliness"—referring to a spiritual workout— for "godliness is of value in every way, as it holds promise for the present life and also for the life to come" (1 Timothy 4:7-8). A Christian woman's life is about bringing her will and every area of her life under submission to God's will.

1 > DISCIPLINE OF THE GOSPEL:
The Source of Godliness

"Christ died for our sins in accordance with the Scriptures" (1 Corinthians 15:3). To be a godly woman you must know what this gospel is, believe it, and make it the center of your life. Never lose the wonder of the gospel. John 3:16 is not only a beautiful summary of what God has done, it ought to be the true center of our living—defining, motivating, and satisfying us. The gospel is a woman's first and most important discipline, for it is the source of godliness.

many Christians don't think Christianly!

In one comprehensive sentence, Paul prescribes his personal mental program: "Whatever is true…honorable…just…pure…lovely…commendable, if there is any excellence, if there is anything worthy of praise, think about these things" (Philippians 4:8). If you are filled with God's Word, your life can then be informed and directed by God—your relationships at home, parenting, career, ethical decisions, and internal moral life.

6 DISCIPLINE OF CONTENTMENT: *Submission's Rest*

Paul wrote from prison that he had "learned in whatever situation I am to be content" (Philippians 4:11). Fortunately for us, he said that he had "learned"… there is hope for all of us who face the monster of discontent!

Applying our knowledge of God to our circumstances is the key to contentment. It will be ours when all that God is and all that he has done in Christ fills our heart. We may lack many things in this world, but as godly women we must work to develop the discipline of contentment.

7 DISCIPLINE OF PROPRIETY:
Submission's Behavior

Propriety means behaving in ways appropriate for Christians—actions that don't bring shame to the Gospel and to Christ. Propriety elevates our words, our appearance, and our attitudes. It's a perfect word for describing what Paul means when he tells believers to act "in a manner of life…worthy of the gospel" (Philippians 1:27).

Propriety means acting in a way worthy of the Gospel in dress (1 Peter 3:3-4), speech, and attitude (Colossians 3:12-14). If your behavior is worthy of the Gospel, the source of that behavior will be a heart authentically bowed in humble submission to Jesus as Lord.

8 DISCIPLINE OF PERSEVERANCE:
Submission's Challenge

Faith in the goodness of God in the face of extreme adversity grows out of a discipline of perseverance in the day-in, day-out grind of everyday life. "Let us run with endurance the race that is set before us" (Hebrews 12:1).

We all can develop perseverance by daily submitting to God's will and looking to Jesus in whatever irritating, insignificant duties or grand-scale tragedies we may suffer (Romans 8:18; Hebrews 12:3). It involves submitting to God in our trials while trusting him to be good, wise, merciful, just, kind, lovingly all-knowing, and all-powerful.

9 DISCIPLINE OF SINGLENESS OR MARRIAGE: *Submission's Framework*

Singleness is a positive assignment (1 Corinthians 7:7) to be joyously received knowing that God doesn't plan to give anyone less than the best. If marriage is our "assignment," then we must discipline ourselves to submit to God's will—to live as our husbands' helpers (Genesis 2:18), submitting to and respecting their position (Ephesians 5:22-24), and developing a gentle and quiet spirit (1 Peter 3:1).

As single or married daughters of Eve—the "mother of all living" (Genesis 3:20)—we must cultivate nurturing spirits. How we care for others will be dictated by where God places us—in a home, in a hospital, in the inner city, wherever.

10 DISCIPLINE OF GOOD DEEDS: *Submission's Industry*

As believers we are "created in Christ Jesus for good works, which God prepared beforehand, that we should walk in them" (Ephesians 2:10). Good deeds are the redeemed heart's response of gratitude for the gift of God's grace (1 Peter 2:12).

We gospel women must determine to develop the discipline of good deeds: "as we have opportunity, let us do good to everyone, and especially to those who are of the household of faith" (Galatians 6:10). Let us fill our days with good deeds.

· ·

As you cultivate the disciplines of godly womanhood, consider Paul's words: "I worked harder than any of them, though it was not I, but the grace of God that is with me" (1 Corinthians 15:10). There is no contradiction between grace and hard work. As we attempt to do God's will, he always gives more grace!

ISBN 978-1-68216-001-5

www.goodnewstracts.org